Why Science Matters

Sports Science

Andrew Solway

Heinemann Library
Chicago, Illinois

Printed and bound in China by Leo Paper Group.

13 12 11 10 09
10 9 8 7 6 5 4 3 2 1

Library of Congress Cataloging-in-Publication Data
Solway, Andrew.
Sports science / Andrew Solway.
p. cm. -- (Why science matters)
Includes bibliographical references and index.
ISBN 978-1-4329-2480-5 (hc) -- ISBN 978-1-4329-2487-4 (pb)
1. Sports sciences. I. Title.
GV558.S63 2008
613.7'1--dc22
                    2008051115

Acknowledgments
The author and publishers are grateful to the following for permission to reproduce copyright material: © Alamy pp. **13** and **21** (Phototake Inc.), **22** (John Fryer), **36** (ImageState), **45** (Moodboard), **47** (Juergen Hasenkopf); © Corbis pp. **6** (Rick Rickman/ NewSport), **11** (Andre Kosters/epa), **14** (Reuters/Kimimasa Mayama), **18 bottom** (Construction Photography), **23** (Christophe Boisvieux), **27** (Lester Lefkowitz), **31** (Toru Hanai/Reuters), **32** (Oliver Weiken/epa), **34** (Reuters), **40** (Tetra Images or Getty Images/Johner Images), **43** (Gilbert Iundt/TempSport); © Getty Images pp. **12** (Bongarts), **15** (Nick Laham), **18 top** (John Gichigl), **25** (AFP), **30** (Photographer's Choice), **37** and **44 bottom** (AFP), **38** (Noah Graham/NBA), **39** (Taxi); © Istockphoto background image and design features; © Jupiterimages **44 top** (Photos.com); © PA p. **10**; © Photolibrary Group p. **5** (Flirt Collection); © Photoshot p. **4** (Bananastock); © Science Photo Library p. **28**.

Cover photograph of man running on treadmill reproduced with permission of © Getty Images/Allsport.

Every effort has been made to contact copyright holders of any material reproduced in this book. Any omissions will be rectified in subsequent printings if notice is given to the publisher.

Contents

Some words are printed in bold, **like this**. You can find out what they mean in the glossary.

What Is Sports Science?

It is the 1995 World Athletics Championships in Göteborg, Sweden. British triple jumper Jonathan Edwards is preparing for his second jump. He breathes deeply, pumping himself up for the effort. Then he explodes into movement, charging down the runway.

Edwards hits the takeoff board and launches into a tremendous hop, step, and leap. He jumps so far that he lands beyond the yellow board marking out the distances. The jump is a record-breaking 18.29 meters (60 feet)! This is still the world record.

Many people join a team to enjoy their favorite sport. Coaches try to improve the athletes' performances. Sports science helps coaches to do this.

During the previous season, Edwards had jumped well, but in 1995 he consistently jumped much farther. One reason for his improvement was a visit to Florida State University in 1994, where sports scientists looked at the **biomechanics** of his jumping. They analyzed carefully how he jumped, looking for areas where his technique could be improved. As a result, Edwards's coach, Dennis Nobles, made changes to his jumping style. This helped Edwards to achieve his world record in 1995.

Sports science and health

Sports and exercise science is not just helpful for athletes. Research shows that people who exercise regularly improve their general health, have a more positive outlook on life, and can live longer. Exercise helps to prevent heart disease and other illnesses, and of course it can help people who are overweight.

A scientific approach

Sports and exercise science was developed to help athletes improve their sports performance. It is the scientific study of exercise and sports training. Scientists focused on two main areas: **exercise physiology** and biomechanics. Exercise physiology is a study of the way the body responds to exercise. It looks at everything from changes in the chemical processes happening in **cells** to whole-**body systems**, such as the **cardiovascular system** (the heart and blood vessels). Biomechanics is a study of the physics of how living things move. It has been used to improve efficiency in sports, such as swimming, and to reduce sports injuries.

Two other areas of science have become important parts of sports training: nutrition and sports psychology. What athletes eat and drink can make a great difference in their performances. Sports psychology is also very important for competition training: it can be the difference between winning and losing.

"I think that at a high level of competition, mental training is important . . . all the riders are similar physically, but it's the mind that makes the difference."

Julien Absalon, four times World Mountain Bike XC champion

One thing that sports science does is to analyze the kinds of fitness that are important for different sports. Basketball, for example, requires agility, quickness, and explosive strength.

THE SCIENCE YOU LEARN: COMPONENTS OF FITNESS

Fitness can be broken down into seven components: power/strength, speed, agility (ability to stop and change direction quickly), coordination, quickness (ability to react quickly), flexibility, and endurance (ability to keep going). Different components are important in different sports.

Think about the sports you enjoy. Which fitness components are most important for each of them? For example, in cross-country running, speed and endurance are most important, while basketball players need agility, power, and quickness.

Movers and Shakers

Before looking at what happens during exercise, we need to look at how the body moves and at the different body systems involved in exercise and sports.

Whenever we move, we use our muscles. They are the body's "movers and shakers." Muscles work in close connection to the skeleton. The bones of the skeleton provide a framework for the muscles to act on.

Contract and relax

Muscles are body **organs** that have the ability to contract, or shorten. Muscles can also relax and lengthen. All our movements are produced by the action of muscles contracting and relaxing.

The muscles we use to move around are called skeletal muscles. This is because they are attached to the bones of the skeleton. As the muscles contract and relax, they move the skeleton.

Sports such as gymnastics test the strength and coordination of the muscles to their limit.

THE SCIENCE YOU LEARN: HOW MUSCLES WORK

Muscles are specialized body **tissues**. They are made up of bundles of long, thin cells called muscle fibers. Each muscle fiber contains a carefully organized arrangement of protein fibers. When a muscle contracts, these protein fibers slide over each other, causing the individual muscle fiber cells to become shorter and fatter. Muscle contraction involves work, so muscles that are working need energy (see page 12).

The biceps and triceps in the upper arm are antagonist muscles. When one is relaxed, the other is contracted.

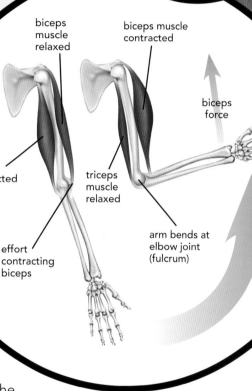

biceps muscle relaxed

biceps muscle contracted

biceps force

triceps muscle contracted

triceps muscle relaxed

effort contracting biceps

arm bends at elbow joint (fulcrum)

Paired up

Many skeletal muscles work in antagonistic pairs. They are called antagonistic because the two muscles work against each other. Generally, if one muscle of the pair contracts, the other relaxes.

The biceps and triceps muscles that move the lower arm are an example of an antagonistic pair. When the biceps muscle contracts, it pulls on the forearm bones to make the arm bend at the elbow. As the arm bends, the triceps muscle relaxes and lengthens.

When the triceps muscle contracts, it pulls on the forearm bones to make the arm straighten. As the arm straightens, the biceps muscle relaxes and lengthens.

In real movements, muscle contraction is never quite this simple. For example, as the biceps contracts to bend the arm, the triceps does not relax completely, but rather maintains a small amount of tension. This helps to make the arm movement more controlled. Other muscles are also involved to stop the elbow joint from wobbling from side to side as the lower arm bends, and to stabilize the shoulder as the lower arm moves.

Cells, tissues, organs, and systems

Muscles are a good example of how the smallest units of the body (cells) are organized into larger units, which are organized into even larger units, and so on. The smallest working units of muscles are individual muscle fibers. Each muscle fiber is a single cell. The muscle fibers are organized into muscle tissue, with blood vessels supplying food and oxygen, and nerves that control when the muscle fibers contract. Each complete muscle is an organ. It is encased in a tough outer membrane and attached either to bone or to another muscle.

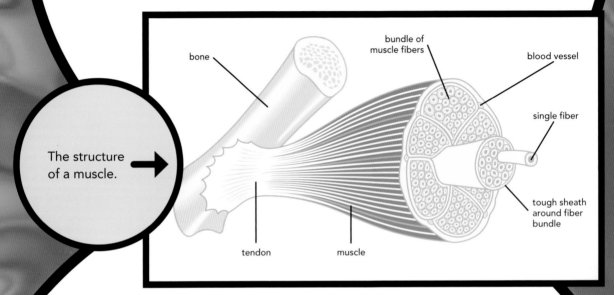

The structure of a muscle.

bone

bundle of muscle fibers

blood vessel

single fiber

tough sheath around fiber bundle

tendon

muscle

Working through levers

The skeletal muscles and the bones of the skeleton together make up the musculoskeletal system. The muscles pull on the bones to make the body move. The bones in the skeleton are jointed, so that the bones can move in relation to each other. The bones and joints together form a set of **levers**. The muscles that work across a joint provide the **effort** needed to move the lever.

Different joints operate as different kinds of lever. The elbow joint, for example, is a lever in which both the **load** and the effort are on one side of the **fulcrum** (see the diagram on page 9). If you are lifting a weight held in the hand, the effort (supplied by the biceps muscle) acts much closer to the fulcrum than the load. This means that the biceps muscle has to produce a large force to lift a light weight. To lift a weight of 5 kilograms, or 11 pounds (49 **newtons**), for example, the biceps muscle must produce a force of about 50 kilograms, or 110 pounds (490 newtons).

Some joints are very complex. The wrist joint, for example, contains eight small bones, all of which can move a small amount, so it does not act as a simple pivot.

THE SCIENCE YOU LEARN: HOW LEVERS WORK

A lever is a kind of bar that can move around a fulcrum, or pivot. If there is a load on the lever, the force needed to move the load depends on how far it is from the fulcrum. It also depends on where the effort (the force used to move the load) is applied. If the load is close to the fulcrum and the effort is far away, the force needed to move the load will be less than the load itself, but the effort will move a greater distance than the load. If the effort is closer to the fulcrum than the load, the force needed to move the load will be greater than the load itself. However, the load will move farther than the effort.

If we look at the lever in the lower arm, the biceps muscle is connected to the lower arm much closer to the elbow (the fulcrum) than to the hand. So, if the arm is lifting a load held in the hand, the biceps muscle, which supplies the effort, has to produce a large force to lift a small load. However, the biceps muscle only has to move a short distance to make the hand move a much greater distance.

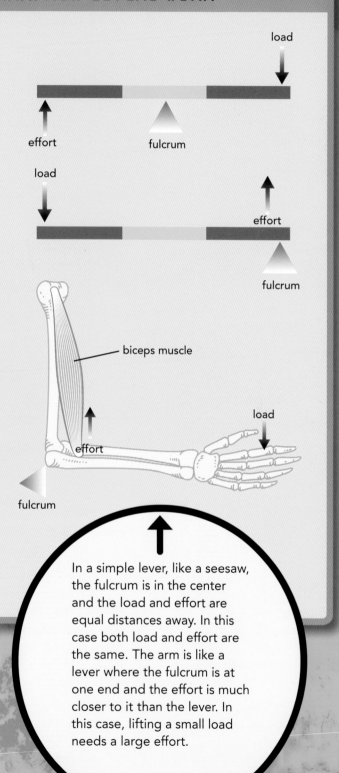

In a simple lever, like a seesaw, the fulcrum is in the center and the load and effort are equal distances away. In this case both load and effort are the same. The arm is like a lever where the fulcrum is at one end and the effort is much closer to it than the lever. In this case, lifting a small load needs a large effort.

9

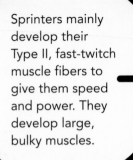

Sprinters mainly develop their Type II, fast-twitch muscle fibers to give them speed and power. They develop large, bulky muscles.

Muscle control

Whenever we move, groups of muscles contract together in a coordinated way. The muscle contractions are controlled and coordinated by the nervous system. Muscles contract in response to signals from the nervous system. The nerves that make muscles contract are called motor nerves. Each motor nerve connects to a group of muscle fibers. When a signal travels down a motor nerve, it produces a contraction in all the muscle fibers it is connected to. In large muscles that produce big movements, such as the muscles in the upper leg, one motor nerve might set off 2,000 muscle fibers. In small muscles that control fine movements, such as those in the hand, each nerve may control as few as 15 muscle fibers. So, when an outfielder leaps for a catch, the movement could involve the same number of nerves as when a pool player adjusts the aim of his cue.

Slow and fast fibers

One important discovery made by sports scientists is that muscle fibers are not all the same. Skeletal muscles contain two main types of muscle fiber, called **Type I** and **Type II fibers**. Type I fibers contract relatively slowly and are not as powerful as Type II fibers. However, they can continue to work for long periods of time. Type II fibers contract quickly and are more powerful than Type I fibers. However, they cannot work for long periods.

Everyone has different amounts of Type I and Type II fibers in their muscles. People with large amounts of Type I fibers will be better at endurance sports, while people with a lot of Type II fibers are better at sprinting and power sports.

Marathon mice

Researcher Yong-Xu Wang and colleagues in La Jolla, California, have **genetically engineered** a mouse that can run up to twice as far as a wild mouse before it gets tired. The genetic change gave the mouse more Type I muscle fibers than ordinary mice.

Studies show that the change in muscle type is connected with special **receptors** in muscle cells. These are sites inside the cell nucleus that can be "turned on" by a particular chemical. When they are turned on, these receptors seem to mimic the effects of exercise training without having to do the training.

Further research may make it possible to make a drug that could produce human "super-athletes." More usefully, an increase in Type I muscle fibers seems to help prevent obesity and to promote general good health.

Endurance athletes mainly develop their Type I, slow-twitch muscles. They are lightly built with long, slim muscles.

Getting Energy

When you exercise, your muscles work hard. They need **energy** to keep going. Muscles can get energy in a variety of different ways. Understanding how the muscles obtain and use energy is central to sports science, because it affects how athletes train for their sport.

Muscle fuel?

All the energy we use comes from food (see pages 28 to 33). Most of the **carbohydrates** in our diet are used for energy. But the actual fuel that muscles use is not sugar or other carbohydrates. It is a chemical called adenosine triphosphate, or **ATP**. Muscle fibers need ATP in order to contract. As they contract, they break down the ATP into another chemical called ADP (adenosine diphosphate). The process releases energy that the muscles can use. Both of these chemicals are produced in the body's cells.

There is only a limited amount of ATP in cells. After an ATP molecule has been broken down to ADP, it needs to be quickly changed back to ATP so that it can be used again.

The energy to change ADP back to ATP can come from several sources. The main one is the complete breakdown of **glucose** to carbon dioxide and water. This process needs oxygen and is called **aerobic respiration**. Except in short, intense bouts of exercise, aerobic respiration is the main way that the muscles get the energy they need to keep working. Exercise and training can improve the body's ability to work aerobically. You can find out more about how this happens in later chapters.

Athletes training on an ergometer can measure their energy output as they train. They might try to keep their output constant at a particular level, or increase their output compared to previous sessions.

THE SCIENCE YOU LEARN:
RESPIRATION

The word *respiration* can simply mean breathing. But, in scientific terms, respiration is also the most important process that happens inside living cells. All living cells, from bacteria to humans, use respiration to get the energy they need to survive. It involves breaking down a sugar (usually glucose) into carbon dioxide and water. The process is essentially the same as burning, but instead of happening all at once, respiration happens in many small stages.

Some of the energy from respiration is released as heat, but most is used to turn ADP back into ATP. Aerobic respiration produces 38 ATP molecules for each molecule of glucose broken down. By contrast, **anaerobic respiration** (see page 14) produces just two ATP molecules per glucose molecule.

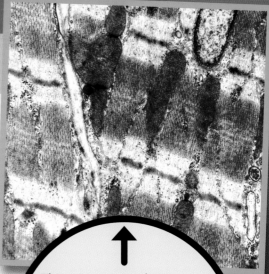

This microscope photo shows mitochondria packed between the muscle fibers in a section of heart muscle. The mitochondria supply the muscles with energy through the process of respiration.

CASE STUDY

Work and power

Any kind of exercise involves energy. Energy is the capacity to do work. Marathon runners use a lot of energy during a marathon because they are working hard for a long period of time. Sprinters in a 100-meter race use far less energy because they are active for only a short time.

Power is a measure of the rate of work—the amount of energy produced per second, minute, or hour. A sprinter produces more power than a marathon runner because he or she uses more energy per second.

In sports science, energy and power output are measured using an ergometer ("work meter"). This is usually a stationary cycle or treadmill, but rowing machines and other devices can also be used as ergometers.

Energy without oxygen

When a muscle is working very hard—for example during a sprint—the muscle fibers cannot make ATP fast enough using only aerobic respiration. So, the muscles partly break down glucose to a substance called **lactic acid**. This process does not need oxygen, so it is called anaerobic respiration.

Although it is fast, anaerobic respiration produces far less ATP than the aerobic process. Also, if lactic acid builds up in muscles fibers, it starts to slow down all the other processes going on there. So, we can only use our muscles at full power for a short time (around a minute). In sprints and other explosive kinds of exercise that last more than a few seconds, the muscles work anaerobically. The body takes several minutes to recover. Lactic acid buildup is one possible cause of muscle cramps. Soccer players sometimes get cramps at the end of a hard match, especially if it goes into overtime.

Peak power

Another fast source of energy is **phosphocreatine** (PCr), a substance found inside the muscle cells. It can react with ADP and re-form ATP very rapidly. However, stores of PCr last only a few seconds.

PCr is important in muscles in two ways. First, muscles produce their maximum power when the energy source is PCr, so it is important in sports where a very short burst of energy is needed. Second, PCr provides energy at the very start of exercise, before other systems to supply energy have kicked in.

"When I actually start to [tire out] I start to lose coordination and judgment and it becomes kind of dangerous. It's totally dependent on whether you've had enough calories."

Juan Lang, triathlete, University of California, Davis

Athletes like this shot-putter work to develop the peak power of their muscles so that they can release the maximum amount of energy in a single explosive burst.

Energy stores

Muscles store energy as **glycogen**, a carbohydrate made up of many glucose molecules joined in long chains. During exercise of more than a minute or two, muscle cells start breaking down their glycogen stores to provide the body with energy via respiration.

Levels of muscle glycogen are important in any long sports event. Marathon runners, for example, sometimes "hit the wall" after about 35 kilometers (22 miles), suddenly becoming very weak and exhausted and sometimes even collapsing. Most commonly this happens when the glycogen stores in the leg muscles are completely used up. The muscles simply cannot get enough energy to keep contracting.

In 2004 British runner Paula Radcliffe failed to finish the Olympic marathon. At 37 kilometers (23 miles) she was unable to go on.

CUTTING EDGE: IMPROVING THEIR GAME

In 1982 Swedish researcher Ira Jacobs and colleagues studied the muscle glycogen levels in top Swedish soccer players. They tested muscle glycogen levels before and after a game and looked at how the players performed during the match. The study found that players with high muscle glycogen levels covered more ground and ran more than players whose muscle glycogen was low, especially in the second half.

Further studies showed that the level of glycogen in the muscles is affected by diet. Eating a diet high in carbohydrates for a few days before a match or race (carbo-loading) boosts muscle glycogen levels. As a result of the investigation, Swedish players changed their diet in the days before an important match. Today, athletes in a variety of sports carbo-load before an important match or competition.

Support Systems

During exercise, the muscles cannot operate alone. They need support from the rest of the body. First, the muscles need a supply of sugars that can be turned into energy. The muscles have some stored glycogen, but this is not enough for an extended period of exercise. Second, the muscles need oxygen. Without oxygen, aerobic respiration cannot happen, and the muscles cannot make the ATP they need to keep them working.

The supplies that the muscles need are brought by the body's main transportation network—the cardiovascular system. The cardiovascular system is made up of the heart, the blood vessels, and the blood itself.

The heart and blood vessels

The heart is the driving force of the cardiovascular system. It is a muscular double pump that pushes blood through two different sets of blood vessels. The left side of the heart pushes blood through the main blood system, which takes blood to the muscles and to other parts of the body. The right side of the heart pumps blood to the lungs (see right).

The blood

The blood does two jobs that are important in exercise. First, it carries glucose to the muscles. Like other sugars, glucose dissolves easily, so it is carried around the body dissolved in the plasma (the watery part of blood). During exercise that goes on for more than a minute or two, glucose from the blood is the main energy source for the muscles.

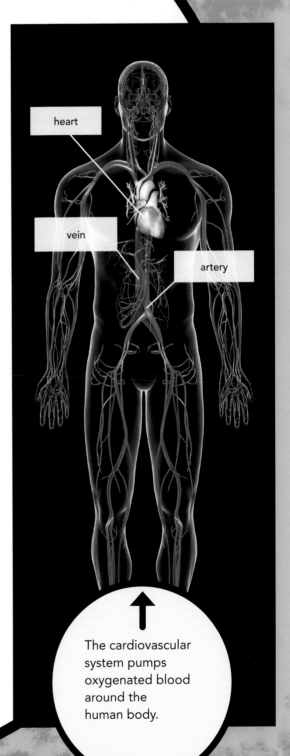

heart

vein

artery

The cardiovascular system pumps oxygenated blood around the human body.

The other important role of the blood is to carry oxygen to the muscles. It also takes away carbon dioxide (carbon dioxide is a waste product of aerobic respiration). Oxygen does not dissolve easily in plasma, so the oxygen is carried instead by the red blood cells. The red pigment (color) in the cells is called **hemoglobin**. It is the hemoglobin that binds the oxygen and carries it around the blood.

THE SCIENCE YOU LEARN: HEARTBEAT

The heart has four chambers: two small ones called atria and two larger ones called ventricles. Each chamber has thick, muscular walls. When the muscles of a chamber contract, it pushes blood out of that chamber.

There are three stages to a heartbeat.
- First, the two atria contract. This pushes blood out of the atria and into the ventricles. Valves prevent the blood from flowing back into the atria.
- Next, the muscles of the ventricles contract. This is a more powerful contraction, which pushes blood out of the heart and into the blood vessels.
- Finally, the whole heart relaxes. This gives the muscles a chance to recover, and the heart can fill up with blood.

The whole process is known as the **cardiac cycle**.

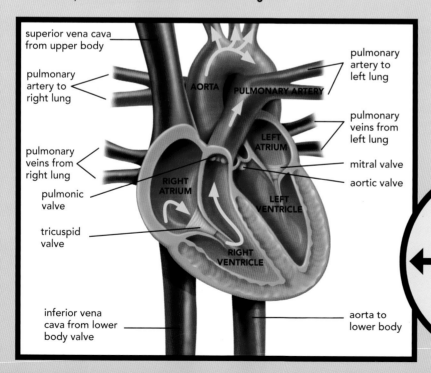

superior vena cava from upper body

pulmonary artery to right lung

AORTA

PULMONARY ARTERY

pulmonary artery to left lung

pulmonary veins from left lung

LEFT ATRIUM

mitral valve

aortic valve

pulmonary veins from right lung

RIGHT ATRIUM

LEFT VENTRICLE

pulmonic valve

tricuspid valve

RIGHT VENTRICLE

inferior vena cava from lower body valve

aorta to lower body

The heart beats about 2.6 billion times during an average lifetime.

Bumping up the blood cells

At high altitude, the air is thinner, so it is harder for the body to get enough oxygen. This makes exercising at high altitude much harder than at sea level. Scientists have shown that people whose families have lived at high altitude for generations are better adapted to cope with low oxygen levels. Their blood contains more red blood cells than normal, which gives their blood extra oxygen-carrying capacity.

Having blood that can carry extra oxygen would be a great advantage for endurance athletes. Some athletes train for a time at high altitude in order to boost their red blood cell count. However, athletes cannot train as hard as at sea level, because exercising at high altitude is so difficult. Also, this training and acclimatization does not permanently adapt the blood—it soon reverts to normal when back at sea level.

These Kenyan athletes are training at a high-altitude training camp in the Rift Valley, Kenya. Many other top endurance athletes also go there to train.

Many exercise machines have a "fat burning" setting, which involves exercising at a lower intensity. Exercising at this intensity does not actually burn more fat. However, the body gets more of its energy from fat during low-intensity exercise, and it is possible to exercise longer. So, a long "fat-burning" session can burn more fat than a short, high-intensity session.

Keeping the sugars coming

In addition to oxygen, the blood needs to carry a constant supply of glucose, or the muscles will run out of energy. This is especially true during exercise, when energy use is high. However, the body cannot store glucose or other sugars. Instead, energy is stored as glycogen, a carbohydrate made up of many glucose molecules joined in long chains.

The main store of glycogen in the body is the liver. When there is too much glucose in the blood (for instance, just after a meal), the liver takes up some glucose and turns it into glycogen. During exercise, when the glucose in the blood is quickly used up, the liver breaks down some of its glycogen to glucose and releases it into the blood.

Muscles first use the glycogen stored in the liver during exercise. Then, the body has to begin using its fat stores to supply the muscles. However, the body cannot burn fats as quickly as sugars. Once the muscles start using fat, the athlete slows down.

CASE STUDY

Blood doping

Athletes desperate to improve their performance sometimes resort to blood doping. Blood doping is not allowed in any sport, but some athletes hope that they will avoid getting caught.

One method of blood doping is for the athlete to have a blood transfusion shortly before a competition. The transfusion increases the numbers of red cells in the blood, so the blood can carry more oxygen. This greatly improves performance in endurance sports.

A newer method of blood doping is to use a substance called erythropoietin (EPO). EPO is a **hormone** found naturally in the body that stimulates the production of red blood cells.

In addition to the risk of being caught cheating, blood doping can have serious consequences for athletes. The extra red cells can make the blood too thick, which can lead to blood clotting and heart failure.

Blood doping has been most widespread in cycling. In the 2007 Tour de France, two complete cycling teams were asked to withdraw because of blood doping, and five other cyclists were shown to have been involved in blood doping of some kind.

The breathing system

The oxygen that the body needs for aerobic respiration comes from the lungs. The lungs allow the body to take in oxygen and get rid of carbon dioxide quickly and efficiently.

Air moves into and out of the lungs through the nose and mouth. Within the lungs is a large, branching network of air tubes, leading to billions of tiny air pockets called **alveoli**. Spread out, the alveoli would cover the area of half a singles tennis court!

Each alveolus is surrounded by a net of blood vessels. These bring the air in the lungs into close contact with the blood, so that **gas exchange** can take place. In gas exchange, the blood takes up oxygen and loses carbon dioxide, while the air in the lungs gets richer in carbon dioxide and loses oxygen.

Lung capacity

During exercise the body needs far more oxygen than at rest. (See pages 14–15 for ways the body can get more oxygen.) But for endurance athletes, who rely on aerobic respiration to keep their muscles working, simply having bigger lungs is an advantage.

Vital capacity is a measure of how much the lungs can breathe in or out at their maximum. Measurements show that in general, endurance athletes have a larger vital capacity than most other people. Four-time Olympic rowing champion Matthew Pinsent, for example, has a lung capacity of 8.5 liters (1.9 gallons), while five-times Tour de France cycling winner Miguel Indurain's lungs have an 8 liter (1.8 gallon) capacity. For comparison, the lung capacity of an average adult male is around 5 liters (1.1 gallons).

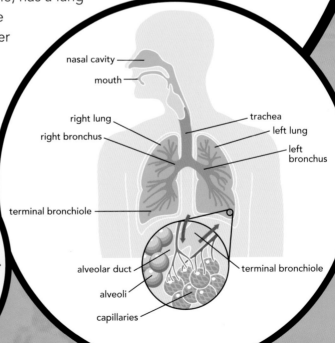

The structure of the lungs. The bronchioles (air passages) get smaller and smaller, then end in air pockets called alveoli.

nasal cavity

mouth

right lung

right bronchus

trachea

left lung

left bronchus

terminal bronchiole

alveolar duct

terminal bronchiole

alveoli

capillaries

How much air do your lungs hold? Find out by testing your lung capacity using a balloon.

You will need:
• round balloons
• a tape measure

Blow the balloon up and then let it deflate. Repeat four or five times, so that it becomes easier to blow up. Then take the deepest breath you can and blow into the balloon until you can breathe out no more. Pinch the end of the balloon to stop the air from escaping. Then use the tape measure to measure the circumference of the balloon (the distance around it at the fattest point). This gives you a measure of your lung capacity.

Do the experiment four or five times and figure out the average of your measurements. Now ask some friends to test their lung capacity with a clean balloon. Who has the biggest lungs?

Lung capacity tests are an important part of the health check carried out on every cyclist before the start of the Tour de France. The three-week cycle race is one of the most grueling sports events in the world. The lung capacity test is done using a spirometer, an instrument used to pick up any problems with the lungs or with breathing.

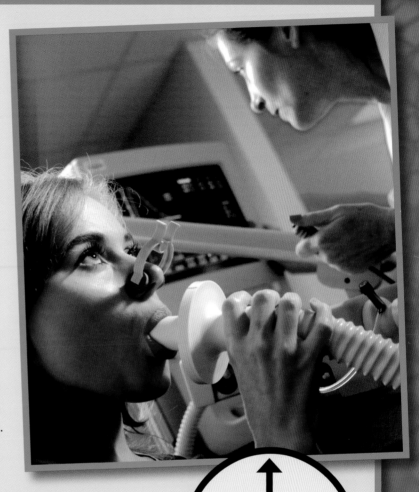

This woman is having her lung capacity measured, using a spirometer.

Responses to Exercise

Anyone who has been in a race will know that the body changes in response to exercise. At the end of a race your chest is heaving and your heart racing. Changes in your breathing and the working of the heart are probably the most important ones that happen during exercise. There are also less obvious changes—for instance, in blood circulation.

At the end of a race, the athlete's body starts to recover from the changes that exercise causes.

Immediate body changes

As soon as you start to exercise, your muscles demand more energy. For a short time your muscles use their own energy supplies, but then the body begins to react. Your breath becomes faster and deeper. More air is drawn into the lungs, and more oxygen gets into the blood. At rest, the lungs draw in about 5 liters (1.1 gallons) of air per minute. During heavy exercise, this can increase to 125 liters (27.5 gallons) per minute in a healthy adult, and even more in a trained athlete.

The heart begins to work harder, too. The heartbeat gets faster, and the **stroke volume** also increases so that the **cardiac output** goes up. This pushes more blood around the body. Cardiac output can increase from 5 liters (1.1 gallons) per minute at rest to more than 30 liters (6.6 gallons) per minute during heavy exercise.

As the blood flows more quickly, the blood vessels taking blood to the muscles open up, while vessels taking blood to other areas, such as the digestive system, close down. In heavy exercise, 85 percent of the blood can flow to the working muscles. However, as exercise goes on, the muscles generate a lot of heat. Blood vessels open up just beneath the skin to help cool the body by losing heat to the outside. The changes in the body mean that the muscles get hugely increased supplies of oxygen and glucose.

CASE STUDY

Fitter than athletes?

Sherpa people live in the Himalayan mountains of Nepal. Many earn their livings as porters, carrying heavy loads for many miles over steep mountain paths. The best weightlifters in the world would have trouble competing with Sherpas in terms of fitness. Exercise scientists studied a group of Sherpas and tested how their breathing and energy expenditure changed when they were carrying loads. They found that the Sherpas could carry a load of up to 20 percent of their body weight without any effect on their breathing or energy use. In comparison, U.S. soldiers carry a maximum of 15 percent of their body weight when on the march. But the Sherpas carry much larger loads than this when they are working. Men carry loads averaging 93 percent of their body weight, while women carry loads of about 66 percent of their body weight. One porter even carried a load that was nearly twice as heavy as he was for 100 kilometers (63 miles), over mountain passes that climb to over 4,500 meters (15,000 feet)!

Nepalese Sherpas are fit enough to carry loads nearly as heavy as themselves for many miles at high altitudes. →

Long-term responses

If you exercise regularly, longer-term changes happen in the body. The kinds of change depend on the kind of exercise. With regular aerobic exercise, the heart slows down because the stroke volume increases—the heart pushes out more blood with each beat. This means that the heart does not have to beat as fast to pump the same amount of blood around the body. A normal, healthy adult has a resting heart rate of around 70 to 75 beats per minute. In a supremely fit endurance athlete, the heart rate can fall much lower. At the height of his fitness in the early 1990s, Tour de France cyclist Miguel Indurain had one of the lowest resting heart rates ever measured—28 beats per minute.

Age	Normal heart rate (beats per minute)
newborn	130
3 months	150
6 months	135
1 year	125
2 years	115
3 years	100
4 years	100
6 years	100
8 years	90
9 years	95
12 years	85
Adult	60–101

This table shows the normal resting heart rate for people from birth to adulthood. It shows how the heart rate becomes slower as we get older.

Another important effect of aerobic training is increased myoglobin in the muscles. Myoglobin is related to hemoglobin (see page 17), which transports oxygen in the blood.

Myoglobin acts as an oxygen store within the muscle fibers and allows the muscles to work harder while still working aerobically. Aerobic training can also improve the breathing rate and the amount of air taken in per breath.

Games such as soccer, football, or hockey involve short bursts of intense activity combined with longer periods of lower-level activity. Professionals need high levels of both aerobic and anaerobic fitness.

Anaerobic training

Anaerobic training is high-intensity exercise in short bursts. The most obvious effect of this is that the muscles get bigger. The muscles begin to bulge because the individual muscle fibers get fatter. They contain more of the special proteins that shorten to make the muscle contract. The capacity of the heart does not grow, but muscles of the heart get bigger and stronger. This happens because during intense exercise the blood pressure rises, forcing the heart to work harder to push the blood through the blood vessels.

Measuring fitness

Sports scientists use various tests to measure fitness. The most common test of aerobic fitness is known as **VO$_2$ max**, which measures the rate an athlete can use oxygen (O$_2$) at maximal exercise intensity. The more oxygen athletes use, the more energy they can produce, so the VO$_2$ max is a very good measure of fitness. However, a correction has to be made for the size of the athlete.

The athlete with the highest VO$_2$ max is not necessarily always going to win races. This is because VO$_2$ max is a measure of maximum exercise output. Athletes cannot operate at their VO$_2$ max for long periods. Their performance depends on what percentage of VO$_2$ max they can work at during a race. Healthy but untrained adults can generally perform at 50 to 60 percent of their VO$_2$ max. Elite athletes can operate at 75 to 80 percent of their VO$_2$ max.

CASE STUDY

Different responses to fitness

The HERITAGE Family Study looked at how different people responded to exercise. One part of the study measured how 742 people who got little exercise responded to a 20-week physical training program. Their fitness levels were tested by measuring their VO$_2$ max before and at the end of the training period. The average increase in VO$_2$ max was 19 percent. However, there was a large variation in people's responses. About 5 percent of people showed little or no change. Five percent had an increase in VO$_2$ max of 40 to more than 50 percent. This large variation occurred at all ages and at all levels of initial fitness.

Recovering from exercise

Sports scientists measure how fast athletes recover from exercise by measuring the levels of lactic acid in their blood at the end of an exercise period. If lactic acid levels are high, this indicates that the athlete will take longer to recover. U.S. Olympic gold-medal swimmer Michael Phelps has extremely low lactic acid levels. After a race, most swimmers have between 10 and 15 **millimoles** of lactic acid per liter of blood. However, after his world record swim at the 2004 Athens Olympics, Phelps had a lactic acid level of just 5.6 millimoles per liter.

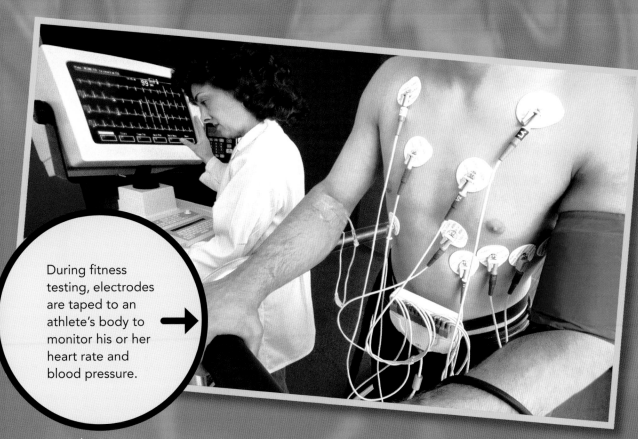

During fitness testing, electrodes are taped to an athlete's body to monitor his or her heart rate and blood pressure.

 INVESTIGATION: TAKING PULSES TO TEST FITNESS

After exercise, the body does not return to its resting state right away. The heartbeat remains high and the breathing is deep. One way of estimating a person's fitness is to test how quickly the heart rate returns to normal after heavy exercise. A fit person will recover quickly from a bout of exercise, while an unfit person will take longer.

For this investigation, you will need:

• a watch with a second hand
• some volunteers to have their fitness tested

First, take each person's pulse at rest. To take a pulse, gently press your index finger on the inside of the person's wrist to find the place where you can feel a regular pulsing under the skin. Count the number of pulses in 15 seconds, then multiply this by four to figure out the heart rate (number of heartbeats per minute). Next, get the volunteer to exercise hard for one minute. A good way is to get him or her to step on and off a bench or step about 45 centimeters (17 inches) high as many times as possible in one minute.

Then, take the person's pulse again. Continue to take his or her pulse at two-minute intervals, until the heart rate falls back to resting levels. The fittest person is the one whose heart rate returns to normal in the shortest time.

Food for Sports

Ultimately, the energy to do any kind of sport comes from food. Like everyone else, athletes need to eat a balanced diet to keep healthy, but need to think even more carefully about what and when they eat. Inappropriate food eaten at the wrong time can significantly affect an athlete's performance at a sports event. For this reason, professional athletes usually have expert medical advisors to monitor their diet.

Carbo-loading

Page 15 describes how glycogen stored in the muscles is important for optimal performance in any sport involving exercise for an hour or more. To make sure that muscle glycogen is at a maximum, athletes should change their training and diet a week before an important competition. At the start of the week, athletes should reduce their training levels but continue with a normal diet. Three days before the competition they should switch to a diet high in carbohydrates and reduce training even further. This is known as "carbo-loading." It gives the muscles a chance to build up glycogen stores to their maximum so that athletes are less likely to suffer from fatigue (tiredness) during long events.

Dietary experts agree that a balanced diet should be high in complex carbohydrates, moderate in protein, and relatively low in fat. →

Right time to eat

Eating at the right time is also important for athletes. On a competition day, athletes should eat a carbohydrate-rich meal at least two hours before the event. This will boost energy levels, but give the food time to digest. If you eat food not long before exercising, blood that could be going to the muscles will instead go to the digestive system. So, eating a meal at the wrong time can significantly affect performance.

Another important time to eat is after training. If athletes eat within 30 minutes of finishing a training session, this leads to improved recovery and encourages muscle development.

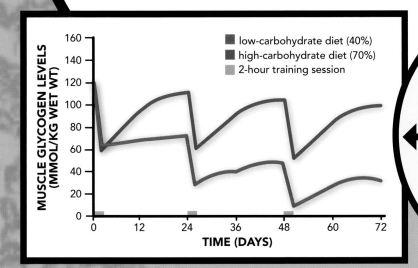

This graph shows how the muscle glycogen levels of an athlete on a low-carbohydrate diet gradually declined over the days of training. In the person on a high-carbohydrate diet, the muscle glycogen recovered to normal every day.

THE SCIENCE YOU LEARN: A BALANCE OF NUTRIENTS

The food we eat is made up of three main kinds of nutrient: proteins, carbohydrates, and lipids (fats). All these nutrients can be used for energy. However, proteins and fats form important structures in the body, and fats are used for long-term energy storage. The nutrients the body normally uses for energy are carbohydrates.

For most people, a balanced diet should contain 40 to 60 percent carbohydrates, less than 30 percent fat, and 10 to 15 percent protein. For athletes the percentage of carbohydrates in the diet should be at least 55 percent. Athletes use more energy than the average person, so they also need to eat more overall.

Food on the go

Taking in extra carbohydrates during a long sports event can improve an athlete's performance. After an hour or more of hard exercise, the body's supplies of glycogen begin to run low. The muscles begin to use fats for energy instead of carbohydrates. Taking in carbohydrates before this happens will keep the athlete's energy levels up and improve performance. Most endurance athletes take in sugars during a race using sports drinks (see page 32).

This athlete is being weighed underwater to determine her body composition. Using this method, sports scientists can figure out how much of the athlete's body mass is fat.

Building up and slimming down

Different athletes need to develop their bodies in different ways. Weightlifters, for example, need to develop their muscles in order to improve their strength. Most athletes perform better if they keep the amount of fat on their body low. Athletes' diets can help them to either build muscle bulk or to lose body fat.

Losing weight might seem simple—you just eat less. But athletes need to be careful. If they eat little, they will lose weight quickly but will have less energy for training, and so their performance will suffer. Athletes should avoid fasting or crash dieting. They should instead reduce their food intake a little and try to increase their exercise schedule, so as to shift their energy balance, the balance between the amount of energy taken in as food, and the amount used doing exercise.

Making weight

Although it is good for an athlete to have fairly low levels of body fat, there are dangers in losing too much weight. Everyone needs some fat, as it is an important energy store. Levels of less than 5 percent body fat in men, and 14 percent in women, can be harmful to health and lead to decreased performance.

Reducing weight too quickly can also be unhealthy. A report from the Irish National Coaching and Training Center looks at the practice of "making weight" in sports such as boxing, weightlifting, and judo, where athletes reduce their weight just before a competition to get into a lighter weight class. The report found that most of the weight loss is either a loss of water or of energy stores in the muscles. This can cause either dehydration (lack of water) or malnutrition (not enough nutrients in the diet). Both these conditions are harmful to health and can lead to poor performance.

Most athletes try to keep the amount of fat on their body to a minimum. Extra fat gives extra weight, which can be an advantage for sumo wrestlers.

In sports such as wrestling and boxing, competitors sometimes lose weight just before a competition by losing water. They do not drink, and they exercise in special suits that make them sweat a lot. However, **dehydration** (having less water in the body) can be dangerous. It can cause heart and kidney problems, and athletes can overheat because they cannot sweat enough to keep cool.

Water loss

Drinking properly is just as important for an athlete as eating well. During heavy exercise, an athlete can lose 2 liters (0.4 gallons) of water per hour, mainly through sweating. Being dehydrated can badly affect an athlete's performance, so it is important to understand water balance during exercise.

The main reason the body needs water during exercise is to keep cool. Muscles produce heat as they work, so in heavy exercise the body produces a lot of extra heat. The main way that the body cools itself is through sweating. As the sweat evaporates, it cools the skin.

Sweat is not pure water: it also contains salt. So, to replace what they lose in sweat, athletes need to take in salt as well as water.

Endurance event athletes need sports drinks with a combination of water, carbohydrates, and salt. →

 SCIENCE AT HOME: MAKE A SPORTS DRINK

Have you ever tried a sports drink? They are sweet, but not as sweet as normal fruit drinks. Most are isotonic, which means that they match the sugar and salt concentrations found in the body. Athletes who drink sports drinks during an endurance event get a combination of water to rehydrate them, carbohydrates to boost energy levels, and some salt to replace that lost through sweat.

Here is a recipe for making your own isotonic sports drink.

You will need:
• 100 milliliters (3.5 fl oz) crushed fruit
• 400 milliliters (13.5 fl oz) water
• a small pinch of salt (be careful: too much salt will stop the body from absorbing the water)

Mix these ingredients in a jug and put it in the refrigerator to chill.

Nutritional aids

Many special kinds of nutrition claim to improve an athlete's performance. Controlled scientific tests show that many of these have no real benefits. However, two substances do seem to have useful effects in some cases. Including extra creatine in the diet seems to increase the amounts of phosphocreatine (PCr) in the muscles (see page 14). The effects of this are mixed, but some people show gains in strength and improved anaerobic performance.

THE SCIENCE YOU LEARN: CONTROLS AND PLACEBOS

People claim that many different drugs, nutrients, and other substances improve athletic performance. Sports scientists use scientific methods to test these claims. In these investigations it is important to have one group of people who take the substance, as well as people in a control group who do not. Often the control group is given a **placebo**—something that looks like the substance, but contains no active ingredients. Strangely, placebos can sometimes have a real physical effect. People think they are being given something that will improve their performance, and their performance does actually improve!

Most good drug trials are double-blind trials: the people involved are randomly assigned to either test or control groups and neither they, nor the researchers doing the test, know who is receiving the drug and who is receiving a placebo.

Improving performance at any cost

Some drugs and other substances can give an athlete an unfair advantage. Most of these substances are banned by sports governing bodies, and some are illegal. However, there are athletes who still use them in pursuit of improved performance at any cost.

Some athletes use illegal anabolic steroids, which mimic the effect of testosterone—a hormone found naturally in the body that encourages muscle development. Anabolic steroid use, combined with exercise, increases muscle and strength development. It can improve performance in sports such as weightlifting, sprinting, and shot put. Steroids, however, have many bad side effects. They can make people very aggressive and sometimes violent. They can also cause damage to the liver and to heart muscle.

Biomechanics

Biomechanics is the study of the physics of how living things move. Human biomechanics can help to improve technique in sports such as swimming, hurdling, and pole vaulting. It has also been used to improve sports surfaces and sports equipment.

David Beckham is renowned for his curving free kicks. A skilled soccer player can curve a shot by giving the ball the right amount and direction of spin.

Analyzing and measuring

Biomechanics analyzes what happens when we make movements and measures the forces and stresses this produces in different parts of the body. The first biomechanics studies looked at simple situations such as standing, lifting, and walking and showed, for instance, that our muscles can exert a maximum force of about 0.3 newton per millimeter squared (N per mm^2). Larger muscles can exert a bigger force because they have a bigger area. For example, a muscle that has a cross section of 5 mm^2 can produce a maximum force of 1.5 N, whereas one with a cross section of 20 mm^2 can produce a force of 6 N. These studies also showed that the faster a muscle contracts, the less force it can produce. This explains why we might manage to lift a heavy weight slowly, but if we try to move it quickly we cannot.

Biomechanics studies look at sports equipment as well as at athletes' bodies. Studies looking at how we throw, kick, or hit balls show that, in theory, the angle to throw or hit a ball to make it go a long distance is 45°. However, this angle can be shallower if the ball has the right spin, and the smoothness or roughness of the ball's surface also has an effect.

 ## THE SCIENCE YOU LEARN: PHYSICS OF SPIN

Studies of good golfers show that they hit long balls at an angle of about 42° rather than 45°, but the ball goes just as far as if it had been hit at 45°. The reason for this is that the ball spins. The face of the golf club is angled slightly backward, so that if the golfer hits the ball well it spins backward as it flies. Spinning backward increases the speed of the airflow over the top of the ball and slows it down beneath the ball. Fast-moving air exerts less pressure than slow-moving air, so the overall effect of the backspin is to give the ball extra lift. The dimples on the surface of a golf ball increase this lift effect.

Air flows faster above the spinning golf ball.

③

Lower pressure above the ball gives it extra lift.

Air flows slower beneath the spinning golf ball.

②

①

The force from the golf club splits into 2 parts.

golf ball

This force drives the ball forward and up.

This force gives the ball backspin.

The physics of spinning a golf ball. Backspin on a golf ball gives it extra lift, so it goes farther.

In other sports, players spin the ball in other ways. For example a tennis player might give the ball topspin (make it spin forward). This reduces the pressure below the ball and increases the pressure on top. The result is that the ball dips sharply toward the ground, then bounces steeply upward. A baseball pitcher may give a ball side spin. The pressure on one side of the ball is greater than on the other, so the ball travels in a curve.

Better equipment

Some sports scientists think that improvements in sports equipment and surfaces are responsible for improved world-record times, more so than improvements in the performance of modern athletes themselves. There is no doubt that better running shoes and tracks have helped athletes to run faster. They have also helped to reduce injuries and long-term damage to athletes' bodies.

While new materials and engineering techniques have made it possible to revolutionize some kinds of sports equipment, biomechanics has played a major role in producing the best designs for this equipment. One example is the design of running shoes. Biomechanics studies of running in the 1970s showed that running shoes were too stiff for inexperienced runners.

The change from wooden to glass- or carbon-fiber poles in 1963 led to an increase in the world record pole-vault height of about 60 cm (23.6 in.) in three years, compared to an increase of just 5 cm (about 2 in.) in the previous 20 years.

CUTTING EDGE: A SPEEDSUIT ADVANTAGE?

In the period leading up to the 2008 Olympic Games, many swimming world records were broken. Nearly all the new records were set by swimmers wearing a particular swimsuit. The Speedo LZR suit was launched in February 2008. Speedo claimed that the new suit reduced drag on the swimmers body by 24 percent, compared to suits worn by swimmers at the 2004 Olympics.

Within weeks, world records began to tumble. Every Olympic swimmer wanted to wear the new suit. At one point, the Japanese swimming team was planning to use a different brand of suit for the Olympics. However, after Japan's Kosuke Kitajima set a new world record in the 200-meter breaststroke wearing the Speedo LZR suit, the team changed its policy and allowed swimmers to wear whatever suit they wanted.

This caused injuries, such as shin splints (pain in the shins caused by muscle and ligament damage in the lower leg). Manufacturers designed shoes with more cushioning. But these shoes gave the foot and ankle less support, which led to ankle injuries. Eventually, a combination of scientific analysis and practical trials has led to running-shoe designs that give both support and cushioning.

Improving performance

Biomechanics studies can help athletes improve their performance by analyzing their technique and suggesting ways to change it. A biomechanical study in the 1970s analyzed the speed of American cross-country skiers and compared it to that of faster teams. It found that the U.S. skiers went just as fast on the flat and downhill, but were slower uphill. The coaches concentrated on improving uphill speed and maximized improvement in the skiers' performance.

Biomechanical analysis can also be helpful in reducing injuries. Some athletes repeatedly get similar injuries, which can be caused by the way they do a particular movement. A biomechanical analysis of their technique can reveal movements that put great strain on a particular joint or body area.

Biomechanical studies have shown that playing a backhand stroke with a flexed wrist is a major cause of tennis elbow in inexperienced players.

Training for Sports

Sports science has had the most effect on how athletes train for their sport. All sports are different, and athletes are different, too. They have different genetic makeups and different characters, and their coaches have different approaches. So, the training regime of each athlete or group of athletes is different. However, sports science has helped to develop a set of basic principles that can be applied to all sports training. These are individuality, specificity, overload, and progression.

Basketball player Jarron Collins stretches before a game. Stretching muscles and ligaments helps to keep the body flexible and reduces the chance of injury.

- **Individuality**: As we saw on page 26, different people have very different responses to the same training regime, so everyone has individual training needs.

- **Overload**: If muscles are to get stronger and develop more endurance, they have to be regularly overloaded. This means pushing the muscles to do more work than they are used to doing.

- **Specificity**: Different sports use different muscles and use them in different ways. So, most of an athlete's training should relate closely and specifically to his or her own sport.

- **Progression**: If you continue a training regime for a week or two, the body will adapt to the regime. To improve, athletes have to change their training to push the body into overload once again. This gradual increase in the demands on an athlete's body is called progression.

Exercise for everyone

The four basic training principles used in sports can apply to any people who exercise regularly to improve their general health and fitness. The two most important are overload and progression. Following the same exercise routine for a long period will not continue to improve fitness. It is important to keep challenging the body and overloading the muscles.

Research shows that getting regular exercise produces many health benefits. People who exercise regularly and eat well are likely to live longer, healthier lives. There is also evidence that exercise helps to prevent illnesses, such as some kinds of heart disease, high blood pressure, and osteoporosis (brittle bones).

Non-sports exercise, such as dance or yoga, is another good way to maintain health and fitness.

CASE STUDY

Jimmie Heuga

In the 1960s, Jimmie Heuga was a talented and successful U.S. skier. In 1964 he won a bronze medal in the Winter Olympics. It was the first medal ever won by a U.S. man in downhill skiing.

In 1970 Heuga found that he had multiple sclerosis (MS). This is an illness in which the body's **immune system** attacks the body, damaging the nervous system. Heuga was advised by doctors not to get any exercise, but after six years he ignored the advice and developed a special exercise program for himself. He found that he felt better both mentally and physically, although exercise did not actually stop the progress of the disease. Heuga set up a center that ran exercise programs and did research into MS. Doctors today agree that exercise is of benefit to people with MS, although it is not a cure.

Resistance training

Athletes participating in any sport that involves strength and power will spend a lot of time doing **resistance training** (exercises using weights or resistance machines). For strength training, athletes should lift large weights relatively few times. For muscular endurance, they should use lighter weights and do more repetitions and sets.

Circuits and intervals

Athletes who need aerobic endurance more than strength may concentrate on circuit training and intervals. They may also do long endurance runs, swims, or cycles.

Circuit training involves doing a "circuit" of several different types of exercise, one after the other, for a set period of time.

Interval training involves doing bursts of fairly intense activity followed by short recovery periods. These bursts can be short, but very intense, to build up anaerobic power, or longer bursts of aerobic exercise.

Resistance training with free weights needs practice and careful supervision to avoid injury.

CASE STUDY

Can you train too much?

A serious college swimmer trained for four hours and swam nearly 14 kilometers (8.7 miles) each day. However, his best time for his main event (200-meter butterfly) was not improving, and he could not get onto the college team.

In the swimmer's final college year, the coach halved his training routine to two hours each day. The swimmer's times improved, and the coach decided to enter him for a race. For three weeks before the race the swimmer's training was reduced even more, to just 1 or 2 kilometers (0.6 to 1.2 miles) per day. In the competition, he got through to the finals, where he came in third with a personal best time.

Periodization

In most sports there is a competition season each year: in some there may be two, or even three, separate seasons. **Periodization** means dividing up the training into periods based on competition seasons or on particularly important competitions. In each period athletes concentrate on a different aspect of their training.

This is the training plan used by U.S. swimmer Michael Phelps in 2000–2001. There are three training peaks and a break in September. Notice how training volume drops in competition weeks.

2000 - 2001
SEASONAL PLAN FOR MICHAEL PHELPS (NBAC)

		SEPT	OCT	NOV	DEC	JAN	FEB	MARCH	APR	MAY	JUNE	JULY	AUG
DATES	MICROCYCLE	1	2 3 4 5 6	7 8 9 10	11 12 13 14 15	16 17 18 19	20 21 22 23	24 25 26 27	28 29 30 31 32 33	34 35 36	37 38 39 40	41 42 43 44 45	46 47 48 49 50
	WEEK BEGINS	Sept 25	Oct 2 / Oct 9 / Oct 16 / Oct 23 / Oct 30	Nov 6 / Nov 13 / Nov 20 / Nov 27	Dec 4 / Dec 11 / Dec 18 / Dec 25	Jan 1 / Jan 8 / Jan 15 / Jan 22 / Jan 29	Feb 5 / Feb 12 / Feb 19 / Feb 26	Mar 5 / Mar 12 / Mar 19 / Mar 26	Apr 2 / Apr 9 / Apr 16 / Apr 23 / Apr 30 / May 7	May 14 / May 21 / May 28	June 4 / June 11 / June 18 / June 25	July 2 / July 9 / July 16 / July 23 / July 30	Aug 6 / Aug 13 / Aug 20 / Aug 27 / Sept 3
CALENDER OF MEETS	INTERNATIONAL / LOCATION		WORLD CUP	XMAS MEET		ATLANTA / WORLD CUP		ALL STAR / W.C. TRIALS	ANN ARBOR	LOCAL SENIO / SANTA CLAR		WORLD CHA	U.S. NATIONAL
PERIODIZATION	TRAINING PHASE	TRANS PERIOD	BUILDING BASE		INTENSITY PHASE	COMP	SPECIFIC	COMP	INTENSITY	SPECIFIC		PEAKING	T
	STRENGTH	REHAB	PROGRESSIVE		POWER	MAINT	PROG / POWER	MAINT	PROG	POWER		MAINTENANCE	M
	ENDURANCE	MAINT	GENERAL PROGRESSIVE		MIXED	MAINT	SPECIFIC	MAINT	MIXED	SPECIFIC		MAINTENANCE	M
	SPEED	MAINT	MAINT		PROG	MAX	PROG	MAX	MAIN / P	PROGRESSIVE		MAX	M
	TESTING DATES												
	MEDICAL CONTROL												
	VOLUME	1 2 3 4 5 6 7 8 9 10	...	...	... 11 12 13 14 15	16 17 18 19	20 21 22 23	24 25 26 27	28 29 30 31 32 33	34 35 36	37 38 39 40	41 42 43 44 45 46 47	48 49 50

VOLUME levels: 100, 90, 80, 70, 60, 50, 40, 30, 20, 10

(BREAK at end)

Before the competition season starts, athletes do preparatory training. The aim of this phase is first to build general fitness, and then to work on technical skill specific to the particular sport. Once the competition season starts, athletes will do less training, but it is more intense and sport-specific. Just before a major competition, athletes will reduce training and go on a high-carbohydrate diet. This allows the body to recover from any tiredness or stress, so that on the competition day the athletes can put in peak performances.

At the end of the competition season, a period of recovery starts. During this time athletes do a minimal level of training, to avoid losing fitness and to give the body time to recover from a strenuous competition season.

Top level training

How does an athlete at the top level train for an event as important as the Olympic Games?

Most top athletes train six or seven days a week and periodize their training to fit in with the yearly calendar of races and competitions. However, training for the Olympics is not part of the normal routine. The Olympics only happen once every four years. They also involve many more sports than at usual competitions.

Heptathlon training

Training for one event is complicated enough, but how does an athlete train for seven? The women's **heptathlon** involves doing seven athletics events over two days—three running events (200-meter, 800-meter, and 100-meter hurdles), two jumping events (long jump and high jump), and two throwing events (shot put and javelin).

Most heptathlon events involve explosive strength, speed, skill, and mobility (flexibility). However, the 800 meters needs aerobic endurance, while the shot put needs absolute strength.

CASE STUDY

Denise Lewis

The British heptathlete Denise Lewis won the gold medal in the heptathlon at the 2000 Sydney Olympics. In 1997 she did 11 training sessions per week, over six days. These sessions included:

- two aerobic runs
- two circuit-training sessions
- one medicine ball session
- two weight-training sessions (resistance training)
- two track sessions
- two technical sessions: one hurdles session and two sessions on other technical events (throwing or jumping), tackling one event in each session.

It takes many years of intensive training for heptathletes to reach their peak. When young people begin heptathlon training, the emphasis is on developing the skills needed for heptathlon events. During this period, they develop the coordination that will form the basis for later development. Once athletes reach a senior level, they begin doing resistance training, to improve their strength and body conditioning. However, most heptathletes need to compete at the top level for several years before they begin to reach their peak combination of fitness and skill.

The U.S. athlete Jackie Joyner-Kersee is probably the greatest heptathlete of all time. She won medals in the heptathlon at three Olympics: silver in 1984, gold in 1988, and gold in 1992. In 1988 she also won Olympic gold in the long jump.

Mental toughness

Physical fitness is not the only kind of preparation needed for the Olympics. Athletes need plenty of competition at the international level to develop the concentration and mental toughness needed to succeed at the very highest level. They also need to eat a balanced diet and make sure that they are eating enough to keep up their muscle energy stores.

Olympic challenge

During the year before the Olympic Games, athletes must reach Olympic qualifying standards. They then compete against others from their own country in national trials. Only the top two or three atheletes in each event at the trials go on to compete at the Olympics. Once an athlete and his or her coach arrive at the Olympic Games, the coach must make sure that the athlete does not lose focus amid the bustle and excitement of the Olympic village. An athlete who can stay focused has a better chance of winning a medal.

All in the Mind

In any competition, many of the athletes have similar levels of fitness and skill. It can be their state of mind that makes the difference between winning and losing.

Sports psychology is the use of psychological techniques to help athletes improve their mindset during competitions. Many top-level athletes employ sports psychologists to help, but all athletes can make use of these techniques to help improve their performance.

Visualizing yourself as a cheetah before a race can help you get in the right state of mind.

 THE SCIENCE YOU LEARN: ADRENALINE

The hormone adrenalin is sometimes known as the emergency hormone, because it prepares the body for action. When adrenaline levels in the blood are high, the heart pumps faster, blood vessels to non-essential areas shut down, and the whole body gears up for action. Just before a competition, an athlete needs to be excited or stressed enough to cause the release of adrenaline, but not so stressed that it impairs performance.

Stress levels

The pressure to win or perform well can make competitions stressful. A certain amount of stress is positive, as it keeps the athlete alert and ready to compete. But too much stress causes worry and loss of concentration. It is important to keep stress at an optimum level—and this varies for different athletes.

Some athletes may reach their optimum performance at high stress levels. They have to "psyche themselves up" before competing. Ways of doing this include a fast and aggressive warm-up to physically stimulate the body, or using images to put themselves into a positive state of mind. For example, a sprinter might imagine himself or herself as a cheetah sprinting down the track. If other competitors do not offer a challenge, athletes can psyche up by setting themselves a personal performance goal, such as finishing a race in a personal best time, rather than just winning the race.

Other athletes perform best at much lower stress levels and use calming techniques before a competition, such as a relaxation routine. They also use routines to focus on what they are going to do in the coming event, rather than worrying about other competitors or whether they are prepared enough.

Concentration is essential. Athletes have to be able to ignore distractions.

Mental qualities

Concentration, confidence, control, and commitment are the four Cs. They are the main mental qualities that are important for successful performance in most sports.

Concentration

Concentration is important in both training and competition to keep focused on the task. Poor concentration in a training session means athletes will get less benefit from training than if they keep focused. In competition, concentration is even more important. Athletes need to be able to focus their whole attention on the event.

Confidence

Confidence is a belief in your own abilities. Having self-confidence means athletes can keep focused when training is not going well, or when they are not doing well in a competition.

Control

Control is the ability to remain calm and focused in the face of distractions. A well-rehearsed pre-competition routine can help athletes remain focused and in control.

Commitment

Commitment is perhaps one of the most important attributes for sporting excellence. Committed athletes are those who stick with their training and competition schedule and keep working toward agreed-upon goals.

SMART goals

Goals are a crucial part of sports psychology. Setting short- and long-term goals and working toward them is the best way for athletes to remain interested and committed to their sport, despite many hours of training that can sometimes be boring or painful.

Setting the right goals is an important skill. The goals an athlete chooses must be SMART:

- Specific: Goals should be clear and concrete, not just vague ideas. A specific goal might be to achieve a particular time in a race at the national championship.
- Measurable: A goal needs to be measurable, otherwise you won't know if you have achieved it.

"It's a challenge for me to beat myself or do better. I try to push out of my mind not what I've accomplished, but what I want to do."

Jackie Joyner-Kersee

- Attainable: Goals should not be set too far out of reach, because it will become discouraging. Scoring a touchdown in the Super Bowl is an unrealistic goal if you are still in high school.
- Realistic: The goal should be based on a realistic assessment of current performance and ability to improve.
- Time-based: A goal should not be something to be achieved at some vague time in the future. Ideally, the goal should be broken down into smaller stages, each to be achieved by a particular point in time.

Where next?

Sports science is a new science that will develop further. There are still many questions to be answered. Why do people react so differently to training? Why are some people more prone to gain weight than others? Will better mental training improve athletes' sports performances? Research by the sports scientists of the future may answer these, and many more, questions.

SCIENCE AT HOME: A TRAINING DIARY

A training and assessment diary is a very useful way of developing the right mental attitudes to do well in sports. The diary should contain records of goals and achievements. It should also include assessments of training sessions or competition performances. A training diary is a record of achievements and progression. Gathering information in a training diary is similar to gathering data in a scientific experiment. As in the scientific method, analysis of the data can lead to useful conclusions about new goals for future training.

Writing a diary of progression and achievements helps to keep athletes focused on their objectives.

Facts and Figures

The following two regimes suggest the kinds of exercise experienced athletes might do, and how their training might progress as they prepare for a competition season. They are not regimes that should be attempted by a young athlete.

The distances that athletes run is always measured in meters and kilometers; 1 meter is equivalent to 3.2 feet.

A training regime for an endurance athlete (10 km runner)

One day per week is a rest day (in this example it is Sunday). The program is arranged in four-week sections. Weeks 1, 2, and 3 get progressively harder, then week 4 is less severe, to allow active recovery and fitness testing.

The actual training program for elite athletes would be tailored to their particular needs.

Weeks 1 to 4

	M	T	W	Th	F	S	S
Flexibility and core stability training.	✓	✓	✓	✓	✓	✓	
Weight training. Emphasis on high repetitions with light loading.	✓		✓		✓		
Medicine ball training and plyometrics (a kind of fitness training that involves a lot of jumping).		✓		✓		✓	
Endurance runs. One of these runs should be fartlek training (alternating hard running with low-intensity jogging/walking).		✓		✓		✓	

The fourth week should include fitness tests to assess progress.

Weeks 5 to 8

	M	T	W	Th	F	S	S
Flexibility and core stability training.	✓	✓	✓	✓	✓	✓	
Weight training. Emphasis on high repetitions with light loading. There should be progression in weight training, based on fitness assessment in week 4.	✓		✓		✓		
Interval training sessions of multiple, shorter runs (for example, 2 x 4,000 meters, or 6 x 1,000 meters) at target race pace, with short rests between each repetition. Distances should increase each week.		✓		✓		✓	

The eighth week should include fitness tests to assess progress. It should also include a VO_2 max session.

Weeks 9 to 12

	M	T	W	Th	F	S	S
Flexibility and core stability training.	✓	✓	✓	✓	✓	✓	
Weight training. Emphasis on high repetitions with light loading.	✓		✓		✓		
Long, fast endurance run, longer than 10 kilometers.					✓		
Longer interval sessions (for example, 2 x 4,000 meters, 4 x 2,400 meters) at best pace.	✓		✓				

The twelfth week should include fitness tests to assess progress.

A training regime for a sprinter (100 m, 200 m, 400 m, sprint hurdles)

This regime suggests the kinds of exercise athletes might do, and how their training might progress as they prepare for a competiton season. The sprint training regime involves three sessions per week.

Weeks 1 to 12

	M	T	W	Th	F	S	S
Technique runs of three to six repetitions of runs between 30 meters and 90 meters (depending on distance being trained for). Repeat this set two to five times. Circuit or weight training for general strength.		✓					
Exercises for specific strength, mobility, and coordination of 30 to 60 minutes. Longer technique runs than on Tuesday (100 to 150 meters).				✓			
Sprinters generally do more than one event. This session should focus on their second event. One session (20 to 30 minutes) special exercises; one or two sets of longer repetition runs (three to six repetitions), 200 to 300 meters.							✓

Weeks 13 to 20

	M	T	W	Th	F	S	S
Sprint speed runs of three to six repetitions of runs between 20 meters and 40 meters, rolling start. Repeat this set two to three times or work on start technique, or acceleration. Circuit or weight training for general strength.		✓					
Exercises for specific strength, mobility, and coordination of 30 to 60 minutes. Repetition runs of two to four repetitions of runs of between 120 meters and 150 meters. Repeat this set one to three times.				✓			
Sprint technique, or 20 minute special exercises for second event, or five runs of 100 meters, 200 meters, 300 meters, 200 meters, and 100 meters. For longer distances, runs could be 300 meters, 250 meters, 200 meters, 150 meters, and 100 meters.							✓

Weeks 21 to 26

	M	T	W	Th	F	S	S
Technique practices last, including relay practice. Two to three runs at full speed over racing distance, with time for full recovery between each run.		✓					
Special exercises and drills for speed and elastic strength. Short sprint speed runs (20 to 60 meters) from blocks, or from rolling start.				✓			
Competition, or technique practices.							✓

Find Out More

Books

Creighton, Jayne. *Science at Work: Boomerangs, Blades, and Basketballs.* Austin: Raintree Steck-Vaughn, 2000.

Fridell, Ron. *Cool Science: Sports Technology.* Minneapolis: Lerner, 2009.

Levine, Shar, and Leslie Johnstone. *Sports Science.* New York: Sterling, 2006.

Morris, Neil. *What Do You Think?: Should Substance-Abusing Athletes Be Banned for Life?* Chicago: Heinemann Library, 2009.

Vizard, Frank. *Popular Mechanics: Why a Curveball Curves: The Incredible Science of Sports.* New York: Hearst, 2008.

Websites

- www.exploratorium.edu/sports/index.html
  This "Sport! Science" website by San Francisco's Exploratorium has features on the science behind many sports, including skateboarding, surfing, baseball, and more. A "Q&A" section offers answers to common questions about sports science.

- http://btc.montana.edu/Olympics
  The National Teachers Enhancement Network (NTEN) created this website to examine how sports science affected the 2008 Winter Olympics. Read about nutrition, physics and biomechanics, physiology and psychology, and more.

- http://wings.avkids.com/Tennis/Project/index.html
  "Aerodynamics in Sports Technology," a part of the educational program of the National Aeronautics and Space Administration (NASA), is a study of sports designed to help students understand sports science. Go to this website to follow a team of scientists as they investigate the science of tennis. Students can collaborate on the website and be a part of new discoveries.

- www.coachesinfo.com
  At the Coaches' Infoservice website, coaches can read up on the latest advances in sports science. Topics such as strength and conditioning are explored in depth.

- www.usaswimming.org
  Most top athletes have their own websites, and there are national websites for most sports. Some are very good—for example, this link for the U.S. swimming team website has interesting news and information.

- www.sciencedaily.com/news/matter_energy/sports_science
  Read about the latest discoveries in sports science at the Science Daily website.

Topics to research

- Find out more about how a ball travels when it is thrown or kicked. What effect does air resistance have? Do other objects, such as the shot or the javelin, move in a similar way to a ball? What about a discus, or an arrow fired from a bow?

- Find out more about core stability and body conditioning. What is pilates? What sort of exercises does it involve?

- Find out more about sports technology. One sport where the technology has changed a lot is cycling. How has the technology changed? What effect has this had on performance?

Glossary

aerobic respiration   process by which the body normally breaks down food to carbon dioxide and water

alveoli   microscopic air pockets in the lungs. Each pocket is called an alveolus.

anaerobic respiration   when cells cannot get enough oxygen, and they get energy from food by breaking it down to lactic acid

ATP (adenosine triphosphate)   chemical in the cell that can provide energy

biomechanics   study of the physics of the movement of living things, and of forces acting on them

body system   group of body organs that work together to carry out a particular function. For example, the respiratory system is composed of the lungs and other organs involved in breathing.

carbohydrate   nutrient such as starch or glycogen that is found in food. Carbohydrates are the main energy foods of the body.

cardiac cycle   one complete contraction and relaxation of the heart

cardiac output   amount of blood that the heart pumps in one minute

cardiovascular system   heart and blood vessels

cell   tiny unit that makes up living things

dehydration   loss of water from the body

effort   weight or force used to move a load

energy   ability to do useful work

exercise physiology   study of the physical changes that occur in the body in response to exercise

fulcrum   pivot point of a lever

gas exchange   process whereby oxygen from the lungs passes into the blood, while carbon dioxide from the blood passes out into the lungs

genetic engineering   changing the genes of an animal or plant for a particular purpose

glucose   sugar that is the main energy supply for cells

glycogen   carbohydrate made in the liver as an energy store

hemoglobin   red pigment found in red blood cells, which carries oxygen in the blood

heptathlon   women's athletic event involving seven different sports over two days

hormone   chemical "signal" that is released into the bloodstream and has an effect somewhere else in the body

immune system   body's system of defense against disease

lactic acid   chemical produced by cells during anaerobic respiration

lever   bar or board that can rotate around a fixed point, or fulcrum

load   weight or force on a lever that is moved by effort

millimole   one millimole is one thousandth of a mole. One mole of lactic acid is 90 grams (3.2 ounces).

newton (N)   standard unit of force. It is the force needed to accelerate a mass of 1 kilogram at a rate of 1 meter^2 per second.

organ   self-contained part of the body that performs a particular job—for example, the heart or the kidneys

periodization   changing an athlete's training schedule to fit in with periods of competition and periods of recovery

phosphocreatine   chemical found particularly in muscle cells that can supply the energy needed to make ATP

placebo   substance given to a patient, who thinks it is a medicine, but which does not have any real effect

receptor   place in a cell where a particular chemical can attach and affect the way the cell works

resistance training   weight training or training using resistence machines

stroke volume   amount of blood that the heart can pump in one heartbeat

tissue   group of similar cells that are organized and work together

Type I fiber   muscle fiber that contracts quite slowly but can keep going for a long time

Type II fiber   muscle fiber that contracts quickly and strongly, but cannot work for long periods

VO$_2$ max   maximum amount of oxygen your body can use in one minute. The higher your VO$_2$ max, the more fit you are.

Index